Detect

and the Case of the Scream Machine

by Daphne Greaves
illustrated by Alan Flinn

Harcourt
SCHOOL PUBLISHERS

Printed in China

ISBN 10: 0-15-351535-X
ISBN 13: 978-0-15-351535-4

Ordering Options
ISBN 10: 0-15-351214-8 (Grade 4 Advanced Collection)
ISBN 13: 978-0-15-351214-8 (Grade 4 Advanced Collection)
ISBN 10: 0-15-358125-5 (package of 5)
ISBN 13: 978-0-15-358125-0 (package of 5)

4 5 6 7 8 9 10 0940 12 11 10 09

Characters

Narrator 1	**Kayla**	**Bob**	**Tansy**
Narrator 2	**Shinto**	**Mr. Kent**	**Adam**

Setting: An amusement park

Narrator 1: This is the story of three friends on an outing at an amusement park.

Narrator 2: They've just come out of the park's Fun House ride.

Kayla: That was really fun! That wasn't scary at all!

Narrator 1: That's Kayla. She just loves thrills and chills.

Kayla: They should have called it the Joke House. I laughed from the minute we entered until the minute we left.

Shinto: Did you know the longest laugh ever recorded was seven minutes?

Narrator 2: That's Shinto. He's a trivia buff.

Kayla: Well, I think I just broke the record.

Shinto: Me, too. I couldn't believe it when Bob asked the scary guy whether they'd met before.

3

Kayla: And then Bob figured it out!

Bob: I realized that the scary guy was the same guy who had been dressed like a mummy earlier.

Narrator 1: That's Kayla's and Shinto's friend Bob.

Shinto: How did you know it was the same guy?

Bob: There were a few clues. They were both the same height.

Kayla: Lots of people are the same height.

Bob: Also, they both used the same exotic cologne.

Shinto: Maybe the scary guy and the mummy shop in the same place.

Bob: I could also see mummy bandages exposed under the scary guy's cape.

Kayla: No way!

Shinto: That is so funny!

Kayla: Even the scary guy thought it was funny.

Shinto: Yeah, he was very gracious about the whole thing.

Kayla: It takes more than a cape to confound Detective Bob.

Narrator 2: Sometimes Kayla and Shinto call their friend Detective Bob. That's because Bob likes to investigate things before making decisions.

Narrator 1: His smile beams self-assurance, and Bob prides himself on being logical and asking questions.

Bob: So what's next?

Kayla: We've got to wait here until my dad gets back.

Narrator 1: Kayla's father, Mr. Kent, is in charge of the group at the amusement park today.

Narrator 2: Right now Mr. Kent is watching Kayla's little brother, Adam, and his friend Tansy.

Narrator 1: They're too little for the Fun House, so they went on the Tea Cups.

Shinto: While we're waiting, let's figure out what ride to go on next.

Kayla: I think we should go on the scariest ride in the entire park.

Bob: Which ride is the scariest?

Kayla: You see that giant ride looming over the amusement park? That's the roller coaster! It's so scary they call it the Scream Machine.

Shinto: Excellent idea!

Bob: What's so scary about the Scream Machine?

Shinto: It's over 300 feet (91.4 m) high.

Kayla: It's an absolutely magnificent machine! I have heard that during the first drop your body bounces straight up in the air.

Bob: That sounds ominous and also rather unpleasant to me.

Shinto: It's also incredibly fast. This coaster reaches speeds of up to 80 miles (128.8 km) per hour!

Kayla: What do you say? Should we go on the Scream Machine?

Shinto: Count me in!

Bob: I think I'll just watch.

Kayla: That's no fun. You've got to come with us.

Shinto: We're a team, participating in everything together.

Bob: It just doesn't sound like a good idea to me.

Kayla: Why not?

Bob: It seems dangerous.

Kayla: No, it isn't.

Bob: How do you know?

Kayla: Oh, boy, Detective Bob is back.

Bob: Before I go on that ride, I want to solve this science mystery. How do you know roller coasters are safe?

Kayla: Well, I don't think the park would have installed the ride if it were dangerous.

Shinto: Did you know that roller coasters date back to the 1600s?

Kayla: That's a long time ago. They must have been able to perfect them since then.

Shinto: Well, they've certainly changed a lot. The first roller coasters were actually made out of ice!

Kayla: You're kidding.

Shinto: No, it's true. People made tall hills of ice. Then they took huge blocks of ice and carved them into sleds. They rode the ice sleds down the ice hills.

Bob: That's a resourceful idea.

Kayla: Brrrrr! I'll bet it was a chilly ride though.

Shinto: Well, they placed blankets on the seats so they wouldn't get cold.

Bob: How did they stop the sleds?

Shinto: They put a lot of sand at the bottom of the hill. The ice sleds would slow to a stop when they reached the sand.

Kayla: You see? It's not dangerous at all.

Bob: Kayla, the Scream Machine isn't made out of ice.

Kayla: I'm absolutely certain that it's safe!

Bob: I don't feel as confident about it as you do.

Shinto: Bob, do you think chewing gum and lawn chairs are safe?

Bob: Of course I do.

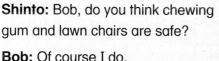

Shinto: Well, more people get hurt from chewing gum and lawn chairs than they do on amusement park rides.

Bob: You just made that up.

Shinto: No, really, I read it in a magazine.

Kayla: So you see, roller coasters are safe.

Bob: That sounds logical. I just wish I understood how they actually work. Maybe then I could make a decision.

Kayla: I know, let's ask my dad about it.

Narrator 2: Kayla's father is a scientist and likes to tinker with machines.

Narrator 1: He knows a lot about how things work.

Bob: That's a great idea. I'll bet Mr. Kent can explain it.

Shinto: Here he comes now with Adam and Tansy.

Mr. Kent: Sorry we took so long. There were a lot of people waiting for the Tea Cup ride.

Tansy: We were almost trampled!

Mr. Kent: Not really. Some people just inadvertently bumped into us. It roused Tansy to direct traffic.

Adam: She told people to make a straight line.

Tansy: That's what we do at school.

Mr. Kent: Anyway, we had a miserable and long wait.

Adam: The ride was worth the wait, though.

Tansy: It spins you round and round really fast. It was fun. You should all go on it.

Kayla: That ride is for little kids.

Adam: Maybe, but it was still fun.

Shinto: Actually, we're thinking of going on the Scream Machine.

Mr. Kent: Are you sure you're all up for thrills, chills, and spills?

Bob: Maybe, if you could answer a few questions for us first, Mr. Kent.

Kayla: Bob's worried the roller coaster isn't safe.

Bob: I'd just like to understand a few things before I decide whether or not I want to go on it. How does a roller coaster work? Is it like a car?

Mr. Kent: That's a good question. Coasters don't have engines. They're pulled to the top of the first hill on the ride. After that, momentum speeds the coaster along. Momentum is the force of the motion of a moving object. Roller coaster tracks are designed so that once the coaster drops from the first hill, its momentum sends it along the entire track.

Bob: What keeps the coaster's momentum from sending it flying off the track?

Mr. Kent: Friction does.

Adam: I know what friction is. That's when you rub something together.

Mr. Kent: That's right, and the greater the friction, the less the movement.

Shinto: That's why if I slide across the floor in socks, I go farther than if I try to slide across it wearing sneakers.

Mr. Kent: Exactly.

Bob: That's interesting, but what does it have to do with roller coasters?

Mr. Kent: Roller coasters have different types of wheels called friction and running wheels. Friction wheels keep the coaster from moving too far from side to side on the tracks. That keeps the coaster from falling off the track. Running wheels guide the coaster along the track.

Bob: What makes the coaster stop at the end of the ride?

Mr. Kent: A couple of things. Roller coasters have airbrakes to safely stop them. The tracks are also designed so that the momentum of the coaster is slowed by the end of the ride. Engineers monitor the design of the ride to make sure it's exciting but safe.

Bob: Thanks, Mr. Kent. I think that cracks the Case of the Scream Machine. We had better go get our tickets!

Adam: Can we go too, Dad?

Mr. Kent: Would you like that, Tansy?

Tansy: Yes!

Mr. Kent: Okay, we'll all go.

Narrator 1: The Scream Machine is very exciting and lives up to its name.

Narrator 2: Bob, Kayla, Shinto, Adam, Tansy, and even Mr. Kent all let out a great big scream.

Everyone: Ahhhh!

Think Critically

1. What is Kayla's opinion of the Fun Ho

2. How does this Readers' Theater help you understand the process of making decisions?

3. What character traits does Bob have?

4. What stops a roller coaster at the end of its ride?

5. What was your favorite part of this Readers' Theater? Why?

 Science

Friction: Good and Bad Shinto said that because of friction, he would slide farther in his socks on a smooth surface than if he were wearing sneakers. Make a list of times when it is good to have friction, such as tires on a road. Then list times when it is bad to have friction, such as a bowling ball rolling down a bowling alley.

 **School-Home Connection** Tell family members about the rides mentioned in this Readers' Theater. Then ask each person to say which ride he or she would most like to go on and why.